THE JOURNEY
Walking the Road to Bethlehem

Youth Edition

THE JOURNEY
Walking the Road to Bethlehem

YOUTH EDITION

Jason Gant

ABINGDON PRESS
NASHVILLE

THE JOURNEY: WALKING THE ROAD TO BETHLEHEM

YOUTH EDITION

This book is printed on acid-free paper.

ISBN 9781426728587

11 12 13 14 15 16 17 18 19 20 —10 9 8 7 6 5 4 3 2 1
MANUFACTURED IN THE UNITED STATES OF AMERICA

Contents

Introduction

The story of Jesus' birth is one of western civilization's best-known stories. It has been immortalized in popular songs, children's Christmas pageants, figurines and lawn ornaments, and great works of art. Even people outside of the church know about the story's setting (a manger in Bethlehem), major players (Mary and Joseph and the shepherds and angels), and overall plot.

But when we take a closer look at this beloved story, we see details that we may have missed. The purpose of this study is to take a fresh look at the story of Jesus' birth by retracing the steps of those who were involved. As you work through the five sessions in this book, you'll take a trip to the Holy Land as it was two millennia ago and examine the key events leading up to and including the first Christmas. Along the way you'll consider what the story of Jesus' birth teaches us about God and our relationship with God. You'll also reflect on how the truths and lessons of Christ's Nativity apply to your life today.

The Purpose of This Study

This 5-session study for teens is inspired by and based on Adam Hamilton's book *The Journey: Walking the Road to Bethlehem.* This study, like the book that inspired it, looks at the events leading up to Jesus' birth in Bethlehem and draws lessons from these events that you can apply to your day-to-day life.

Also Available

- *The Journey: Walking the Road to Bethlehem,* by Adam Hamilton (ISBN 9781426714252)
- *The Journey: Walking the Road to Bethlehem* DVD, including a leader guide (ISBN 9781426719998)
- *The Journey: A Season of Reflections,* a devotional companion (ISBN 9781426714269)

Although this resource is intended for teens, the book itself is set up like an adult Bible study. Whether a leader or a participant, everyone has the same book and literally is on the same page. Leaders should review the material in advance to determine which activities and discussion questions the group will use.

The Journey: Walking the Road to Bethlehem Youth Edition includes five sessions, making it ideal for the season of Advent (one session for each Sunday during Advent, plus one session for Christmas Sunday). But the impact of the Nativity story is not limited to a certain time of year. Regardless of the season, this study is a great way for youth Sunday school classes or Bible study groups to gain a better understanding of what Mary, Joseph, and the other persons in the story experienced in the days leading up to Jesus' birth.

Each of the five sessions includes the following parts:

Getting Started—Each session identifies a few goals for that session. These goals give leaders some clear teaching objectives and participants something to focus on as they journey with Mary and Joseph from Nazareth to Bethlehem. Each session also provides definitions of key words and place-names that may be unfamiliar to many participants.

Introduction—While none of us have been told by an angel that we will give birth to or parent the Messiah, we can still draw from our experiences to gain a better sense of what Mary, Joseph, and the other players in the story of Jesus' birth were experiencing. Every session's introduction makes a connection between an event leading up to Christ's birth and a situation that most young people today find familiar. Participants can read the introduction prior to each session, or groups can spend time reading the information during each session.

Testimonial—Every session includes an interview with a young person whose personal experience mirrors what is going on in that session's Scripture passage.

Video Presentation and Discussion—An optional, but recommended resource, Adam Hamilton's *The Journey* DVD takes viewers to the Holy Land, where he visits sites that are traditionally associated with the events leading up to Jesus' birth. Each of the segments runs about 10 minutes. Each session provides a list of sights (what viewers will see on the DVD) and key insights (what viewers should take away) for that session's video segment. The session also provides a list of discussion questions that groups can use to debrief the video.

Book Study and Discussion—This part of the session is also optional. Because this study is based on Adam Hamilton's *The Journey,* participants would benefit from reading and reflecting on that book. Every chapter in the book corresponds to a session in this study, and each session provides questions for groups wanting to discuss and debrief what they have read.

Bringing the Scripture to My Life—One of the main objectives of this study is to help participants make connections between the events leading up to Jesus' birth and their lives today. This part of each session provides discussion questions that help participants make these connections.

Going Deeper in Truth—While the primary Scripture for every session is a Gospel text related to Jesus' birth and promised coming, other Scriptures give us insight into the significance of who Jesus is, why Jesus came to live among us, and what we can learn from the events surrounding his birth.

Experience Life in Community—Jesus and his closest followers were a tight-knit community. They traveled together, ate together, learned together, and forgave one another. Jesus' followers throughout history have maintained this emphasis on community, and life in community is an important part of each session.

Making It Personal—Belonging to a community of believers is an essential part of the Christian life, but the gospel also has an impact on us as individuals. Every session gives individual participants instructions for putting what they've learned into action during the coming week.

Closing: Listening for God—Every session concludes with a time of prayer and reflection, lifting up what the participants have learned and asking God's guidance as everyone goes forth.

What we really hunger for will not be found under the tree on Christmas morning. We hunger for meaning, for joy, for hope in the face of despair. We hunger to know that we can be forgiven and start anew after things we regret. We hunger for a love that will not let us go and for life and triumph in the face of death. These come through a baby born in a stable, laid to sleep in a feeding trough, visited by night-shift shepherds. He is for us the bread of life. And we must come to the stable to satisfy the deepest desires of our hearts.

I invite you to come to the manger this Christmas and to eat of this bread. I invite you to choose to become Christ's follower and to put your trust in him. John tells us that "all who received him, who believed in his name, he gave power to become children of God" (1:12, NRSV).

Christmas is the perfect time to call out to God and to his son Jesus Christ and to pray, "Jesus, I come to you, like the shepherds and the magi did so long ago. I accept you as my King, my Savior, and my Lord. Forgive me for the ways I've turned from God's path, and help me to follow you. Save me from myself, and help me to live for you. I receive you, Jesus Christ, and believe in your name. Make me your child, and bring me your joy. Help me to do justice, to love kindness, and to walk humbly with you. In your name I pray, Jesus my Christ. Amen."

—Adam Hamilton, *The Journey: Walking the Road to Bethlehem*

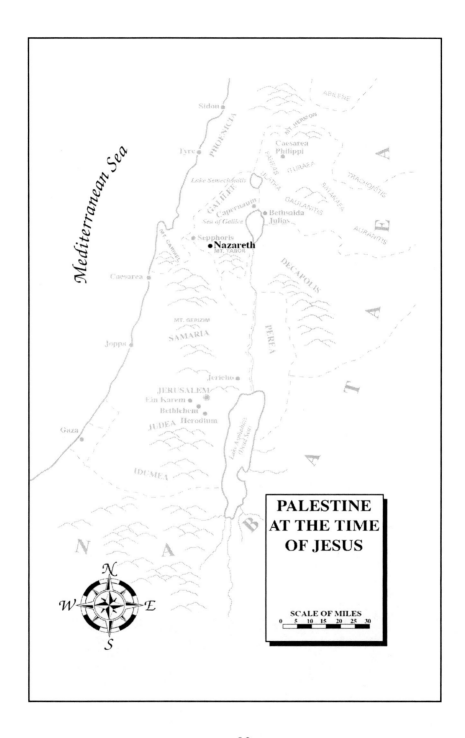

Session 1:
Mary's Story

Getting Started

Goals for This Session

—Claim that God is love and desires to share that love to and through each of us.

—Learn and understand what the Annunciation meant for Mary and for each of us today.

—Explore what it means to be called by God.

Words to Know

Annunciation: a divine announcement

Calling: a nudging toward serving God

Confirmation: a rite through which a young person learns the essentials of the Christian faith and has an opportunity to affirm his or her faith and "confirm" his or her baptism

Introduction

You know that feeling you get when someone important unexpectedly calls you by your name? You find yourself thinking, wondering, even being amazed that the person who called your name knows who you are! I'm not speaking of that girl or guy you've been crushing on since school started. I'm talking about something bigger and more powerful than that "special crush" who may have noticed you. I'm talking about the God of all creation! A moment when the all-powerful, all-loving, all-forgiving, almighty God calls you by name? Imagine both joy and fear, maybe even "jear"—joy with just enough fear to remind you to treat the moment with such respect so as to not mess it up! This is what Mary may have felt during what we refer to in big, fancy, church language as the "Annunciation." God called Mary by name. Wow!

Read the following paraphrase of Luke 1:26-38 from *THE MESSAGE*:

> In the sixth month of Elizabeth's pregnancy, God sent the angel Gabriel to the Galilean village of Nazareth to a virgin engaged to be

married to a man descended from David. His name was Joseph, and the virgin's name, Mary. Upon entering, Gabriel greeted her:

Good morning!
You're beautiful with God's beauty,
Beautiful inside and out!
God be with you.

She was thoroughly shaken, wondering what was behind a greeting like that. But the angel assured her, "Mary, you have nothing to fear. God has a surprise for you: You will become pregnant and give birth to a son and call his name Jesus.

He will be great,
    be called 'Son of the Highest.'
The Lord God will give him
    the throne of his father David;
He will rule Jacob's house forever—
    no end, ever, to his kingdom."

Mary said to the angel, "But how? I've never slept with a man." The angel answered,

The Holy Spirit will come upon you,
    the power of the Highest hover over you;
Therefore, the child you bring to birth
    will be called Holy, Son of God.

15

"And did you know that your cousin Elizabeth conceived a son, old as she is? Everyone called her barren, and here she is six months' pregnant! Nothing, you see, is impossible with God."

And Mary said,

Yes, I see it all now:
    I'm the Lord's maid, ready to serve.
Let it be with me
    just as you say.

Then the angel left her.

Let's begin by remembering why God created us in the first place: God is love. We know this from Jesus' life, teachings, sacrificial death, and resurrection. Also, there are many stories in Scripture where we see God's deep love for us shine through. Since God is love, it makes sense that God would desire to give away that love or to be in loving relationship with others. God created us to be in relationship with God and to share that loving, meaningful, powerful relationship with all people. As our relationship with God grows, we begin to understand more and more the hopes and dreams of God!

Scripture tells us that, when Mary first heard God's call, she was understandably shaken. To have the Creator of the universe call her by name, then tell her she was "beautiful with God's beauty," reminded Mary that she had been created in the very image of God. Then to be told she would become pregnant by the power of God's Spirit and that the child would be called Holy, the Son of God—well, you might imagine that she felt the full force of God's power—both joy and fear.

Then Mary does something remarkable. She responds with humility in service to God!

Testimony: Kaitlyn's Story

Recently I talked with Kaitlyn, who is sixteen years old and has felt God's call to be a youth pastor, and asked her a few questions.

JASON: Explain for me the moment at which you felt God's call to be in ministry.

KAITLYN: The moment I heard God's call I was sitting and reading the Bible. While I was reading, I was asking God for some guidance, because I felt I needed something to push me. Paul [in 1 Corinthians 12:1-11] says some are called to be pastors, some teachers, and so on. I immediately felt God was calling me personally into ministry. It's like it was something I was meant for and the words in the Scriptures were speaking directly to me. I felt my life was going in the direction of becoming a youth pastor. I began to notice certain people and resources that seemed to be sent by God to help me!

JASON: Wow, what a moment! Had you had any feelings about ministry before that?

KAITLYN: Yes. I felt it when my confirmation small group all pointed at me when Adam [Senior Pastor of Church of the Resurrection, where Kaitlyn attends and where I serve on staff, and author of *The Journey: Walking the Road to Bethlehem*] asked who in the group should become a pastor. My class pointed at me, and I was scared and excited!

JASON: When did you first feel that you understood who God is?

KAITLYN: At vacation Bible school when I was a kid. I remember learning that God is good and God created us. Then later in fifth grade, while at basketball camp at my church, I gave my heart to God.

JASON: Have you ever doubted that you "have what it takes" to be in ministry?

KAITLYN: Yes, but then I remember stories about Mary and others in which God called regular people, even people who had no education or had made major mistakes in the past. Then I think I can do it with God's help. God will make me strong for God's call!

I listened to Kaitlyn talk about her calling, and I learned what Mary may have felt that day. How important it would have been for Mary to completely trust God through her call and resolve to remain strong even when she felt doubt.

Bringing the Scripture to My Life

- Have you ever felt God calling you, whether to ministry or to a specific task, in your day-to-day life?
- How does God speak to people today?
- How does knowing that God is love shape your understanding of what love is meant to be? How can we love God and others as Jesus commanded us?
- How have we (meaning people in general) misrepresented what love is meant to be?

- Read "Kaitlyn's Story." How can you relate to her experience of receiving God's call?
- How have you heard God's call? Has anyone ever told you that you may have a calling to serve God in a specific way? Have you prayed to God about what God may be calling you to do? Did you receive an answer? If so, what did you hear?

Taste and See (Optional)

In the Jewish world during the late first century B.C., where Mary lived, the women often started their day by making bread. They began by grinding grain, and they crushed the grain between stones in small, hand-operated mills to make flour.

Grinding grain, using the tools that were available in Mary's day, is no easy task. Give it a try.

✶ LEADERS: Set up a grinding stone: Place a stack of newspapers on the floor. On top of this stack of newspapers, place a flat rock or wooden cutting board. Sprinkle millet seed, barley kernels, or wheat kernels on the cutting board or flat rock.

Participants should take turns using a round rock to smash the seeds or kernels on the flat rock or board. Smashing the seeds or kernels will produce flour that can be used to make bread.

After grinding the grain to make flour, things got a little easier. The women would add water and yeast to the flour to make dough. They would knead the dough for about an hour and then make the dough into thin, flat loaves about the size of a dinner plate.

✶ LEADERS: Give each participant a ball of biscuit dough and some waxed paper. Tell them to put some flour on their hands, then invite them to knead the dough into a thin, round disk. When finished, place the flattened disks on a baking tray. Bake them according to the instructions on the package and serve them as a snack after baking.

Video Presentation and Discussion (Optional)

Watch the video segment "Mary's Story," from *The Journey* DVD. (Running Time: 9:19 minutes)

SIGHTS

- An old Roman road leading from Sepphoris to Nazareth
- The Greek Orthodox Church of the Annunciation in Nazareth
- The spring in Nazareth that provides water for the village and was the reason people settled there so many years ago
- The Roman Catholic Church of the Annunciation in Nazareth that was built on top of caves
- A five-room cave near Jerusalem where one or two ancient families lived
- The Basilica of the Annunciation in Nazareth, which is built over a grotto where, according to tradition, Mary lived and first heard the news that she would give birth to Jesus

KEY INSIGHTS

Sepphoris, near Mary's hometown of Nazareth, was a city of thousands that had existed for hundreds of years and was a hub of Hebrew and Greek culture. The people of the village of Nazareth were poor when compared to their neighbors in Sepphoris. Many of them likely traveled to Sepphoris to work and shop, but they lived a much different lifestyle from those they encountered in the big city. People settled in Nazareth because it was home to a water source: a spring that provided the village "living water."

Nazareth's name likely comes from the Hebrew word for "branch" or "shoot." Several centuries earlier Isaiah used the image of a branch or shoot to talk about a ruler who would bring justice and righteousness. Adam Hamilton reads from a passage in Isaiah that talks about a shoot "from the stump of Jesse." Jesse was David's father. The person about whom Isaiah wrote would be a descendent of David, Israel's greatest king.

The people in Nazareth were peasants who were looked down on by their wealthier neighbors. We see evidence of this in John 1:46, where Nathaniel says, "Can anything from Nazareth be good?" God chose a village peasant girl who was considered insignificant by most to be the mother of the Messiah.

- What do we learn from this story about the character of God?
- What does this story teach us about Mary, and through Mary, about God's will for our lives?
- What does this story teach us about the child to be born to Mary?

Book Study and Discussion (Optional)

Prior to this session, read the first chapter of *The Journey: Walking the Road to Bethlehem*, by Adam Hamilton. Use the following questions to discuss this chapter with your group:

- What did you learn from this chapter about Mary's hometown of Nazareth?
- Why is the natural spring that still flows today so important to the town of Nazareth? Why was it important to Jesus' ministry?
- What did you learn from this chapter about Mary's life and upbringing?
- What does the Hebrew word *netzer*, which may have given Nazareth its name, mean? Why is this meaning significant?

- To whom or what were the prophets of ancient Israel and Judah referring when they wrote about the "branch" or "shoot"?
- What did you learn from this chapter about God and how God works?

Going Deeper in Truth

The Annunciation is one of many examples from Scripture in which God calls someone. Here are some others to read and discuss:

The call of Moses: Exodus 3:1–4:17
- What did God call Moses to do?
- How did God speak to Moses?
- How did Moses respond?
- What about Moses' call do you identify with?

The call of Gideon: Judges 6:11-24
- What did God call Gideon to do?
- How did God speak to Gideon?
- How did Gideon respond?
- What about Gideon's call do you identify with?

The call of the Jesus' first disciples: Luke 5:1-11
- What did Jesus call his disciples to do?
- How did Jesus call his disciples?
- How did his disciples respond?
- What about the first disciples' story do you identify with?

The call of Lydia: Acts 16:11-15
- What did God call Lydia to do?
- How did God reach out to Lydia?

- How did Lydia respond?
- What about Lydia's call do you identify with?

Experience Life in Community

✷ LEADERS: Gather the participants in teams of two or three.

Work with your team to write and present a commercial to promote answering God's call. Think about the qualities and characteristics of someone who answers God's call. Be humorous and creative.

✷ LEADERS: Invite each team to perform its commercials. Then discuss the following questions.

- What do these commercials teach us about how God calls us and how we should respond?
- What type of people do we expect God to call?
- What do we know from Scripture (and from our personal experience) about the type of people God calls?

Making It Personal

Often there are two reasons why people don't respond to a call from God:

1. They believe that God isn't truly speaking to them.
2. They believe that they aren't worthy of God's call.

However, time and time again, God has called unlikely people—people whom others surely considered unworthy, even ordinary. Moses was a fugitive who had committed murder; Rahab was a prostitute; Paul had hunted down and persecuted Christians; Mary was young and unmarried.

Any of these people could have argued that he or she was unworthy (and Moses actually did). But God had other ideas.

What reasons have you given God for not responding to God's call? In the space below, list excuses you have given (or could imagine yourself giving) for not responding to God's call. Then mark through each one, as a symbol of eliminating the excuse and releasing you to fulfill God's dreams!

Closing: Listening for God

Gather in a circle for a "jear" (joy + fear) prayer. Your leader will begin the time of prayer, thanking God for the opportunity to come together and reflect on God's call. Allow anyone who feels led to say words that describe his or her fears about being called by God. After an appropriate amount of time, anyone who feels led may also say words that describe the joys of being called by God. A leader will close the prayer, perhaps using the following words:

Lord, we all have fears and we all dream of new joys. May we be content and trusting, just as Mary was before us, that you will work your power through both fears and joys! Amen.

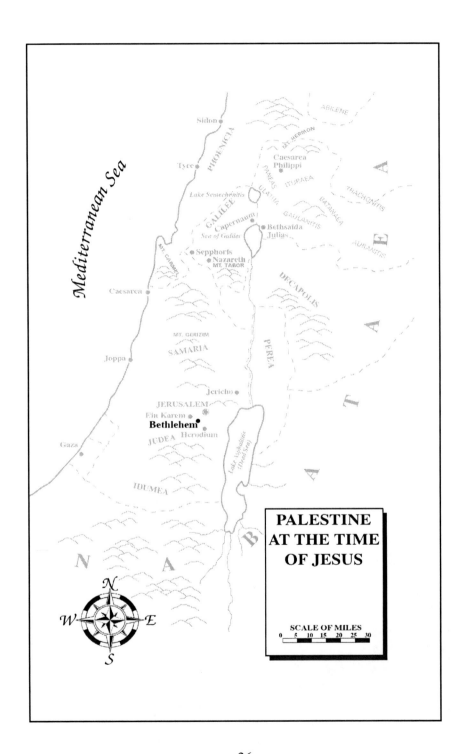

Mediterranean Sea

Sidon

PHOENICIA

Tyre

MT. HERMON

Caesarea
Philippi

ABILENE

PANEAS

ITURAEA

TRACHONITIS

Lake Semechonitis

ULATHA

BATANAEA

GALILEE

GAULANITIS

Capernaum

Bethsaida
Julias

AURANITIS

Sea of Galilee

Sepphoris

Nazareth
MT. TABOR

DECAPOLIS

Caesarea

MT. GERIZIM

SAMARIA

PEREA

Joppa

Jericho

JERUSALEM

Ein Karem

Bethlehem

JUDEA

Herodium

Gaza

Lake Asphaltitis
(Dead Sea)

IDUMEA

N

A

B

A

T

A

E

A

N   W   E   S

**PALESTINE
AT THE TIME
OF JESUS**

SCALE OF MILES
0   5   10 15   20 25 30

Session 2:
Joseph of Bethlehem

Getting Started

Goals for This Session

—Learn how God—in the person of the Holy Spirit and through Scripture—gives us courage along the journey.

—Explore God's challenge to Joseph to stay faithful to God and true to Mary.

—Discover ways in which we can have the courage to become young men and young women of God.

Words to Know

Accomplice: a person who joins with another in carrying out some plan (especially an illegal or unethical plan)

Peer pressure: the influence exerted by a peer group in persuading a person to change his or her attitudes, values, and/or behavior to conform to the group

Introduction

Have you ever felt that your own decisions were beyond your control? What I mean is this: Something happens that was not, in any way, a personal choice you made, yet you feel all the weight and judgment of what happens. Perhaps people look at you differently because of a decision made by a family member or close friend. They identify you with that decision and its consequences, even though you had nothing to do with it. They brand you as an accomplice.

Have you ever heard the saying, "You are who your friends are"? There is some truth to this statement. We all are influenced by the people who are closest to us. Whether we realize it or not, these relationships shape us. That's why it's so important to ask ourselves this question:

> Do my friends point me upward toward Christ, or do they point me away from a relationship with him?

This question forces us to think critically about whom we allow to influence us. Here's an even more important question:

> Am I the kind of friend who points people upward toward a life with Christ, or am I the kind of friend who pulls people downward?

Jesus' desire is for us is to choose to be in relationships that honor him, that help both persons make decisions as Jesus would make them, and in which both persons support each other and grow in faith.

Take Joseph. Joseph and Mary are engaged to be married. As we learned in the previous session, Mary answers God's call to give birth to the promised Messiah, placing her in a unique and touchy situation. She must tell Joseph, her husband-to-be, that she is pregnant and that the child in her womb is the Son of God. Then Joseph has a choice to make.

Read the following from Matthew 1:18-25, from the Common English Bible (CEB), a new translation combining scholarship and readability.

This is how the birth of Jesus Christ took place. When Mary his mother was engaged to Joseph, before they were married, she became pregnant by the Holy Spirit. Joseph her husband was a righteous man. Because he didn't want to humiliate her, he decided to call off their engagement quietly. As he was thinking about this, an angel from the Lord appeared to him in a dream and said, "Joseph son of David, don't be afraid to take Mary as your wife, because the child she carries was conceived by the Holy Spirit. She will give birth to a son, and you will call him Jesus, because he will save his people from their sins." Now all of this took place so that what the Lord had spoken through the prophet would be fulfilled:

> *Look! A virgin will become pregnant and give birth to a son,*
>   *And they will call him,* Emmanuel.
> (*Emmanuel* means "God with us.")

When Joseph woke up, he did just as an angel from God commanded and took Mary as his wife. But he didn't have sexual relations with her until she gave birth to a son. Joseph called him Jesus.

These verses tell us a powerful story about trust in God. People would surely assume that Joseph and Mary had conceived a child out of wedlock or that Mary had been unfaithful to her fiancé. Joseph could have saved both of them a lot of grief if he had quietly called off the engagement. But he didn't. He remained faithful to God and to Mary. Joseph's decision shows that he was a man of courage and conviction and that he trusted God in a way that was stronger than any judgment the world could bring on him. This speaks greatly to Joseph's character as a man of God and as a soon-to-be husband and father.

Testimony: Phillip's Story

Recently I asked a young man I know named Phillip about character and integrity. Phillip is eighteen years old and a senior in high school.

JASON: Phillip, what does it mean to be a man of character?

PHILLIP: To me a man of character is someone whom a freshmen or a sophomore can look up to and wants to be like. Everyone goes through tough times. When you have someone to look up to, you think, *I can make it through this because he or she did too.*

JASON: Do you believe young men fall into temptation out of a fear of judgment?

PHILLIP: It comes down to peer pressure! This has happened to me and to a lot of my friends. Peer pressure is so powerful and it can affect your integrity. They may have a lack of judgment and get talked into something they know they shouldn't be doing, because they think that everybody else is doing it.

JASON: What do you think God expects from you in the midst of that pressure?

PHILLIP: God has given me this life, and I think God wants me to live my life to the fullest for him. God wants me to be a representative for faith, not just with my words but also my actions. He gives me love, mercy, and compassion even after I do stupid stuff. God wants me to build Christian community here on earth.

JASON: What are ways you fight against that pressure?

PHILLIP: The number one way is my boys (my small group). We call ourselves "The God Squad." I have been with these guys since eighth grade, and we have two volunteer adult leaders who have been with us since we started. My small group of guys helps me have trust in God and gives me advice. Hanging around together has helped us become stronger in our faith!

Bringing the Scripture to My Life

- Read "Phillip's Story." What, do you think, does Phillip mean when he says, "to live my life to the fullest for God"?
- What does it mean to trust God? How can you live out your trust in God through your everyday decisions?
- What steps can you take to surround yourself with friends who lift you "up" toward Christ? What opportunities do you have to participate in small groups of supportive Christian friends (such as the group you're meeting with right now)?

- Joseph and Mary had the courage to face any criticism or judgment that came their way because they trusted in God. How can you grow stronger in your trust in God? What life situations are you currently experiencing that require great trust in God's guidance?

Taste and See (Optional)

In first-century Palestine, meat was a luxury for many people. Much of the land was used for agriculture, leaving little room for pasturing animals. A carpenter such as Joseph likely would not have been able to afford meat. He and his family would have lived mostly on a diet of grains, fruits, and vegetables.

★ LEADERS: Provide a snack of fruits and vegetables that Joseph might have eaten—such as dates, figs, and cucumbers—along with some pita bread. Consider making a simple cheese-and-yogurt dip for the bread and cucumbers: Mix together 6 ounces of feta cheese, two cups of Greek-style yogurt, 2 tablespoons of dill, 2 tablespoons of chopped parsley, and 2 tablespoons of mint.

Video Presentation and Discussion (Optional)

Watch the video segment "Joseph of Bethlehem," from the *The Journey* DVD. (Running Time: 12:16 minutes)

SIGHTS
- The well of Bethlehem that we read about in 2 Samuel 23:15
- The Herodium, a mountainous monument built by King Herod the Great, just outside of Bethlehem, including a 900-seat amphitheater and the king's palace on top of the hill

- The toolbox used by Adam Hamilton's grandfather, who—like Joseph—was a carpenter

KEY INSIGHTS

The town of Bethlehem had a rich heritage as King David's home city. The prophet Micah said that God's Anointed One would come from Bethlehem.

Bethlehem means "house of bread" and was home to many wheat and barley farmers.

The Gospels tell us little about Joseph, and there is nothing written about him outside of the Gospels. We know that he made his living by building things. There are different traditions about Joseph's age. Some imagine that he married Mary when he was very young, possibly fifteen years old. Other traditions say that Joseph was an elderly man, a widower with children from a previous marriage.

According to the law, Mary—who was engaged but who had appeared to have become pregnant by someone other than the man she was engaged to—could have been put to death by stoning. Joseph, out of mercy and righteousness, wouldn't allow this to happen to her.

Joseph, like the Joseph in the Book of Genesis, heard God in dreams. And Joseph was always obedient to what God revealed to him in dreams. He lived a life of true greatness through mercy, obedience, and humility.

King Herod the Great stands in "stark contrast" to Joseph. Herod built an enormous monument to himself just outside of the town where Joseph worked as a humble carpenter.

- What do we learn from this story about Joseph and the city of Bethlehem?
- What do we know about Joseph from the few verses in the Bible that mention him?

- Why, do you think, did God choose Joseph to be the earthly father of Jesus?
- What can we learn about greatness from Joseph's story?

Book Study and Discussion (Optional)

Prior to this session read the second chapter of *The Journey: Walking the Road to Bethlehem*, by Adam Hamilton. Use the following questions to discuss this chapter with your group:

- What did you learn from this chapter about Joseph's hometown of Bethlehem?
- Why was Bethlehem an important town in the history of God's people?
- What does the Bible tell us about Joseph?
- What do we know about Joseph from his work as a carpenter?
- How did Joseph respond to the news that Mary was pregnant?
- What happened to Joseph on his journey back to Bethlehem from Nazareth?
- What is Matthew telling us about Jesus when he refers to Jesus as "Emmanuel"? Why does Matthew refer to Isaiah 7:14 to tell us about Jesus?
- What did you learn from this chapter about King Herod the Great, who was king at the time of Jesus' birth and for much (and maybe all) of Joseph's life?
- How was Joseph different from King Herod? Why is the difference between these two men so important?

Going Deeper in Truth

There are many stories of trust in the Bible. Here are two stories about young people who trusted in God. Read and discuss:

Daniel 3:1-30—Shadrach, Meshach, and Abednego

- Shadrach, Meshach, and Abednego were willing to trust God even if God didn't "save them from the fire." What would it take for you to have that kind of trust in God?
- How significant or different was their trust in God, knowing they were facing it together (as a small group) instead of alone?

Daniel 6:1-23—Daniel and the Lions' Den

- We learn in this Bible passage that Daniel received much of his strength through prayer. How can you grow in your personal prayer life by listening to and trusting in God?

Experience Life in Community

✶ **LEADERS:** Pair up participants so that each person has a partner. Create a walking course with a starting and ending point, some twists and turns, but not too many obstacles.

Learn and practice trust and accountability by taking a "lean walk." The goal is for you and your partner to walk from Point A to Point B while leaning into each other's shoulders (so much so that your bodies make an inverted 'V' shape). Lean just enough that you would fall without each other's support. To finish the course, you and your partner will need to rely on and support each other.

After this exercise, discuss the questions on the following page:

- What did this activity teach you about trusting your partner?
- What did this activity teach you about supporting your partner?
- How do you "lean on" and trust God?
- How can you support others as a Christian friend?

Making It Personal

There are many reasons that doubt creeps in and causes us to question our faith and trust in God. You may have found yourself testing God at times. For example:

"God, if you give me an A on this test, then I will always trust you."

"Jesus, if you are truly there, then turn this red light to green."

These kinds of thoughts actually indicate a lack of trust in God. Paul writes in Philippians 4:13:

"I can do all things through [Christ] who strengthens me" (NRSV).

In the space provided on the next page, list the areas of your life (*school, sports, church, family, friends, and so forth*) where you most strongly feel God's presence. Then list the areas where you struggle to feel God's presence. Now, beside each area where you struggle to feel God's presence, list something you can do to invite God into those parts of your life (for example, *say a prayer before practice, worship together as a family, join a weekly Bible study or small group, and so on*).

Areas where I most strongly feel God's presence:

Areas where I struggle to feel God's presence and ways I can invite God into these parts of my life:

Closing: Listening for God

Refer back to "Making It Personal" (page 36) and select one area of your life where you strongly feel God's presence and one area where you struggle to feel God's presence.

★ LEADERS: Gather everyone in a circle. Go around the circle, and ask each person to say one word that describes each of these two areas of his or her life (where he or she strongly feels God's presence and where he or she struggles to feel God's presence), without giving any details. Then close the circle prayer with these words:

Lord, you know the places in our lives where we feel your strength, and we thank you for your presence in those places. Lord, you also know the places where we need your strength. We invite you into those places to fill us with trust and faith so that these places become one in our hearts and lives this week. Amen.

When we look at Joseph, we are meant to see God's call to humble service and obedience. Most of us want to be like Joseph—to serve God and others and to do so selflessly and without regard for recognition and affirmation....

Joseph models for us how to serve without expectation of reward. He had the most important job ever given to a man up to that point. His was the task of raising Jesus and teaching him how to be a man. He did this without recognition, without the praise of others, solely because God called him in a dream to care for God's Son.

Adam Hamilton,
The Journey: Walking the Road to Bethlehem

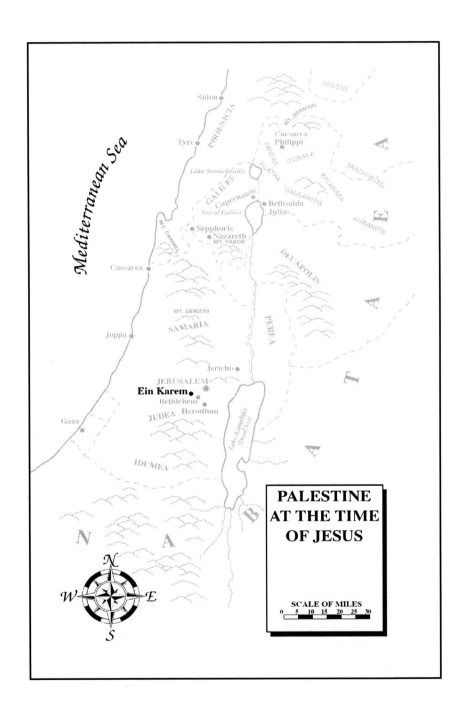

PALESTINE
AT THE TIME
OF JESUS

SCALE OF MILES
0 5 10 15 20 25 30

Session 3:
Mary and Elizabeth

Getting Started

Goals for This Session

—Recognize that we are blessed with family, friends, and mentors who
guide us along our journey of faith.

—Learn how healthy mentoring relationships can strengthen our walk
with Christ.

—Discover that what may seem like the worst thing is never the last
thing!

Words to Know

Prophet: an inspired teacher or messenger of God's will

Prophecy: a vision of what can, should, or will happen in the future

Introduction

Ever needed a word of encouragement or simple assurance that things are going to be OK? That a decision you've made will work out or that a circumstance you find yourself in will be manageable? Even when we're certain that a decision was the correct one, we often seek immediate assurance. We might end sentences with the word *right?*, hoping that others will nod in agreement and lessen our insecurities. It is especially assuring when we learn that someone else has had similar doubts or been in similar circumstances. We need someone who can say, "I've been there, and I've done that, and I'm OK." The testimony of someone who has gone through what we're going through is much more meaningful than any textbook advice a person might offer.

While we know that Mary was fully committed to God's call, she likely found herself in need of assurance from a trusted friend or family member. She may have sought that extra nudge or nod to let her know that everything would be OK.

In Luke 1:39-45 Mary, who has just learned that she is pregnant with God's Son, travels to visit her relative Elizabeth, who is in the sixth month of pregnancy.

> Mary got up and hurried to a city in the Judean highlands. She entered Zechariah's home and greeted Elizabeth. When Elizabeth heard Mary's greeting, the child leaped in her womb, and Elizabeth was filled with the Holy Spirit. With a loud voice she blurted out, "God has blessed you above all women, and he has blessed the child you carry. Why do I have this honor, that the mother of my Lord should come to me? As soon as I heard your greeting, the baby in my womb jumped for joy. Happy is she who believed that the Lord would fulfill the promises he made to her."

In this account of Mary's visit to Elizabeth, some exciting things happen:

1. Mary visits a loved and trusted relative who is older and more experienced.
2. Elizabeth's child, who would grow up to become John the Baptist, jumps in his mother's womb, as if to say, "the Savior is here!"
3. The Holy Spirit, through Elizabeth, confirms Mary's blessedness and calling from God.
4. Elizabeth refers to Mary as "the mother of my Lord."
5. Elizabeth tells Mary that she is "blessed" (or "happy") because she "believed that the Lord would fulfill the promises he made to her" (verse 45).

During what surely had to be a difficult and uncertain time for Mary, this experience gave her encouragement, support, and assurance that God was with her.

Testimony: Matt's Story

I have known Matt and his family for five years and am honored to be a mentor in his life. Matt is now sixteen years old. Recently I asked him about something he experienced when he was ten years old that could have driven him away from God if not for the encouragement, support, and assurance of his family and church family.

JASON: Matt, what happened in your life when you were ten years old?

MATT: It was 4:00 A.M., and I woke up and heard my mom running all around the house. She was clearly upset and told me to go back to bed. Then an ambulance came and, the next thing I knew, some friends of our family were taking my brother and me to the hospital. That's when my mom told us that my dad had died suddenly. He had a heart attack in his sleep and passed away. He was gone.

JASON: What did you feel at that moment when you learned about your father?

MATT: Doubt and disbelief. I thought for sure the doctors had made a mistake. When my mom started crying, it became real. I began to wonder what would happen now: How would our family continue? What would I do? I didn't sleep for many nights because of worry.

JASON: How did you continue? What did you do next?

MATT: I had a really good friend who knew I wasn't sleeping well and who invited me over to stay with him for a few nights. Hanging out with him helped take my mind off of the stress. I also had an awesome mentor who had worked with me during confirmation at church in seventh grade and whose son had passed away. I thought to myself: *If he can get through it and be such a man of faith, then I can get through it too.* That was when I began to realize that God was with me through my caring friends and great leaders at church.

JASON: What about now, Matt, after six years? Do you see God with you?

MATT: All the time! Through sharing my story, hanging out with my friends and leaders at church, and trusting that God has a plan for my life. My mom gave me a drum kit, and I started playing in the worship band and at youth group. Leading worship has helped me grow stronger and stronger in my faith. There are times when I am sad that my dad's not here, but having so many people who care about me reminds me that God loves me no matter what.

I have watched Matt grow and discover gifts that God has given him to use as a witness to God's love. Time and time again his family and his church family have come together through a difficult journey. Matt's faith and trust in God is still growing. He still has moments of sadness, but the Holy Spirit navigates him through those difficult times. You may have also experienced challenges or struggles, or even just feelings of anxiety. During these times remember Mary's commitment and resolve to do God's will. Also remember Matt's belief that God is always with him.

Bringing the Scripture to My Life

- Read "Matt's Story." Have you ever been through a struggle or challenge that you would be comfortable talking about with the group?
- How was God present with you during this time? How has God continued to be present with you?
- God offered Mary assurance through Elizabeth. How has God offered you encouragement and support through other people?
- How do you manage stress, anxiety, and/or pressure in your day-to-day life? In what ways can we give our burdens, fears, and worries to God?

Taste and See (Optional)

Mary's older relative Elizabeth lived in a town called Ein Karem, a village near Jerusalem whose name means "spring of the vineyard." The grapes that grew in Ein Karem's vineyards were eaten fresh, dried into raisins, or used for making wine.

★ LEADERS: Lead the group in making a snack with raisins that is similar to Halvah balls, a treat that was common in biblical times.

You will need wax paper, 1/2 cup of raisins, 4 ouncces of pitted dates, 4 ounces of dried apricots, 1/2 teaspoon of cinnamon, between 1 and 2 tablespoons of lemon zest, between 1 and 2 tablespoons of lemon juice, a mixing bowl, measuring cups and spoons, mixing spoon, and cookie sheets.

Pour chopped raisins, dates, and apricots into a large mixing bowl. Add cinnamon and lemon zest. Mix all of the ingredients together. Add enough lemon juice so that the mixture sticks together. Using the mixture, make small balls and place the balls on wax paper. Serve and enjoy these Halvah balls as a snack during your time together.

Video Presentation and Discussion (Optional)

Watch the video segment "Mary and Elizabeth," from *The Journey* DVD. (Running Time: 9:03 minutes)

SIGHTS

- The village of Ein Karem, where Mary's relative Elizabeth is believed to have lived
- The Church of the Visitation, built on top of a grotto that is said to have been the home of Elizabeth and Zechariah
- Assorted works of art showing the meeting of Mary and Elizabeth
- Children living in poverty who have been blessed by Christmas offerings

KEY INSIGHTS

The journey from Nazareth to Ein Karem was a difficult, ten-day journey. Mary made this trek in hope of finding answers—or at least a sympathetic listener.

Elizabeth served as a mentor for Mary, offering encouragement and affirmation for her younger relative. After Elizabeth offered Mary words of comfort and support, Mary launched into song, singing the verses we know today as the "Magnificat" (from the first line, "My soul magnifies the Lord"). This song praises God for lifting up the humble, the brokenhearted, and the hungry. God calls us to participate in God's work by showing mercy to these people.

The Christmas season should be celebrated not by lavishing expensive gifts on ourselves but by reaching out to those who are poor and hurting.

- What do we learn from this story about the challenges Mary faced?
- Why did Mary visit Elizabeth? How did Elizabeth encourage Mary?

- Who are some adults, other than your parents, with whom you can talk when you are having a difficult time or facing a tough situation? How have these adults offered you guidance and support?
- What does Mary's song, the Magnificat, tell us about God and God's priorities?
- What are some ways that you can show love and mercy to the people Mary lifts up in her song (the lowly and the hungry)?

Book Study and Discussion (Optional)

Prior to this session read the third chapter of *The Journey: Walking the Road to Bethlehem*, by Adam Hamilton. Use the following questions to discuss this chapter with your group:

- What did you learn from this chapter about Mary's relationship with Elizabeth?
- Why, do you think, did Mary make the long journey from Nazareth to Ein Karem to visit her older relative?
- How did Elizabeth respond to Mary's visit?
- How did Elizabeth help turn Mary's fear into joy?
- What does it mean to be "blessed"? Can we be blessed and still face struggles and challenges? Explain.
- Who is your "Elizabeth"? Who is an older person (other than a parent) who gives you guidance and support?
- Who is your "Mary"? Who is a younger person who looks to you for guidance and support?
- Why are mentoring relationships important? How does God bless us through these relationships?
- What is the theme of Mary's song of praise, the Magnificat? What does this song reveal about Christ?

- What does this chapter say about ways that we could change our Christmas celebrations?
- How can you change your Christmas celebrations to help people who are hungry or living in poverty?

Going Deeper in Truth

The Gospel writers who wrote about Jesus' life found many prophecies that anticipated the coming of Jesus. Matthew (see 1:23) cites Isaiah 7:14 when he writes:

> *Look! A virgin will become pregnant and give birth to a son,*
> *And they will call him,* Emmanuel.

Isaiah 7:14 referred to a sign given to Ahaz, King of Judah, during an especially difficult time in the nation's history. The name "Emmanuel" (or "Immanuel") means "God is with us." Matthew tells us that, in Jesus, God was with God's people in an incredible new way.

Discuss the following questions:

- How have you experienced signs from God?
- Why was Jesus called "Emmanuel," or "God is with us"? How was God with us in the person of Jesus? How is Jesus still with us?

Isaiah, in a later message of hope for the people of Judah, writes, "Trust in the LORD forever, for in the LORD GOD you have an everlasting rock" (Isaiah 26:4, NRSV).

Discuss the following questions:

- What does it mean for God to be our "everlasting rock"?
- When you, like Mary and Matt, face a major life challenge, how will you trust in God as your "everlasting rock"?

Experience Life in Community

✶ LEADERS: Assemble the participants in groups of four or five. Instruct each group to follow the instructions below.

In your groups, spend a few minutes thinking about the other people in your group. Ask yourself, *What are the gifts, talents, and positive qualities of each person in this group?* After everyone has had plenty of time to think, go around the circle, pausing at each person, while the other members of the group name two or three of that person's good qualities. Explain that when each person receives the compliments, he or she should not respond nor should the person discount or deny the good things that people say about him or her. Tell each person to simply accept the words he or she hears.

✶ LEADERS: Allow several minutes for the youth to exchange compliments. Then bring everyone back together and discuss the following questions:

- How did it feel to receive words of encouragement from your friends?
- Did you learn anything new about yourself in this exercise?
- How would our lives be different if we made more of an effort to give one another encouragement and assurance?

Making It Personal

This week think of one person in your life who has given you encouragement and has been a positive influence. This may be a family member, a teacher, or some other person. Take the time to call or text this person or leave a note on his or her Facebook wall thanking him or her for the support, encouragement, and assurance he or she has offered you.

Also, write this person's name in the space below as a reminder to pray for him or her.

Closing: Listening for God

★ LEADERS: Gather the participants in a circle. Go around the circle and ask each person to think of one person in his or her life who could use some words of encouragement, assurance, and support. No one needs to call out names; saying "a friend" or "a teacher" or "a relative" will suffice. Suggest that whoever says the closing prayer should lift up these people, then ask for a volunteer to pray the following prayer:

Lord, thank you for calling Mary and giving her the incredible responsibility of giving birth to your son, Jesus. Thank you also for Elizabeth, who was available to give Mary support and assurance. Just as you called Mary and Elizabeth, we know that Jesus calls us to make disciples and to offer assurance to our neighbors. Lord, we lift up [say names aloud]. Guide us so that we are encouraging and supportive to them and may we always point them toward your faithfulness and love. Amen.

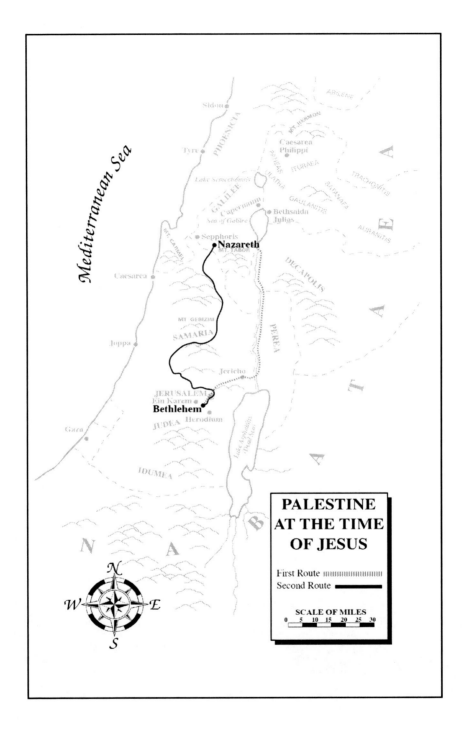

Session 4:
From Nazareth to Bethlehem

Getting Started

Goals for This Session

—Recognize that God walks with us in the valleys of our life journey.

—Learn that God is our Creator, and God invites us into God's story.

—Discover that we each have gifts and experiences that will shape our strengths and courage.

Words to Know

Messiah: literally means "Anointed One"; refers to the promised and expected Savior of God's people

Registration, or census: an official count of the population of a city, nation, or region

Manger: a feeding trough in a barn or stable from which livestock such as cattle eat

Introduction

Have you ever had a "mountaintop experience"? Mountaintop experiences are moments when you feel especially close to God or strong in faith. These moments might include summer camp, a youth group mission trip, a Christian concert, baptism, or confirmation.

Mountaintop experiences are great, and they remind us who we are as children of God and followers of Christ. But it's important that we develop the kind of faith that not only sustains us when we're on top of the mountain but also that is strong enough to handle the valleys.

Life is a journey. As with any journey, the terrain is not always easy. Each of us faces obstacles and hazards. At times we may feel lonely, abandoned, exhausted, overwhelmed, or stuck. The good news is that we do not face these struggles alone. We have Christ by our side.

Jesus' birth surely was a "mountaintop experience" for Mary and Joseph. They knew that the child would be God's Son, the Messiah. But they also had to traverse some difficult terrain. We've already discussed some of the emotional struggles that Mary and Joseph may have faced. But the registration, or census, that took place toward the end of Mary's pregnancy meant that the couple would have to make a difficult physical journey, traveling from Mary's hometown of Nazareth to Joseph's hometown of Bethlehem. The trip would have taken about ten days. Mary and Joseph likely traveled with a caravan. Each night the caravan would have needed to stop somewhere near a water source. The second half of the journey, through the hills and mountains of central Israel, would have been particularly difficult, especially since Mary was several months pregnant. In addition to the challenges of making the ten-day trek, Mary also faced giving birth far away from home in a strange city, and where she didn't know a midwife.

What might Mary and Joseph have been thinking as they made this journey from Nazareth to Bethlehem? What questions might they have asked?

> Is God really with us?
> Why do we have to go through all of this?
> Why is God allowing this to happen?
> Is this really part of God's plan?

When Mary and Joseph arrived in Bethlehem, the struggles continued. There was no place for them to stay except in a stable. (The stable may have been in a cave next to Joseph's family's home.) And after Mary gave birth, her newborn child had to sleep in a manger—a feeding trough for livestock. Could this truly have been part of God's plan—that the Messiah be born in a barn?

Difficult circumstances, such as those Mary and Joseph faced, can try our faith. But it is possible to find faith during troublesome times. We can experience God's love and presence in ways that aren't apparent when times are good. Read Luke 2:1-7 and reflect on the challenges Mary may have faced while making a difficult journey so late in her pregnancy.

In those days Caesar Augustus declared that everyone throughout the empire should be enrolled in the tax lists. This first enrollment occurred when Quirinius governed Syria. Everyone went to their own cities to be enrolled. Since Joseph belonged to David's house and family line, he went up from the city of Nazareth in Galilee to David's city, called Bethlehem in Judea. He went to be enrolled together with Mary, who was promised to him in marriage and who was pregnant. While they were there, the time came for Mary to have her baby. She gave birth to her firstborn son, wrapped him snugly, and laid him in a manger, because there was no place for them in the guestroom.

What did it mean that in God's plan Jesus would be born in a barn and sleep in a manger among the animals and their mess? Was it God's plan to send us a message that faith can be found in life's valleys?

Testimony: Ashley's Story

Ashley is eighteen years old and has been on quite a journey. I asked her some questions about that journey and how it has affected her faith.

JASON: Ashley, tell me about your life the past few years.

ASHLEY: I was diagnosed with OCD (obsessive-compulsive disorder) when I was eight years old. In the past few years the disorder continued to get worse, and then I just stopped functioning—didn't talk with my friends, felt depressed all the time, woke up screaming at night, and I worried all the time. I worried that God didn't love me and that I wasn't good enough. And I began to doubt that God was real. It was very difficult!

JASON: It sounds difficult. What happened next?

ASHLEY: My parents checked me into a treatment center in 2009. That's when I began to gain control again and everything began to change. I had a lot of time to reflect and I began to read the Bible. I felt Jesus speaking to me through my reading. I began listening to Christian worship music that inspired me and gave me a sense of peace.

JASON: You said something powerful to me when I asked if you wanted to share your story. Do you remember what it was?

ASHLEY: Yes, I said that Jesus saved me and saved my life!

JASON: Tell me more about that.

ASHLEY: Well, I see my OCD . . . as a distortion. Something I must face but not "who I am." With Jesus and his power I can face this head on. I'm not alone!

JASON: What else have you discovered about who you are through this?

ASHLEY: I've learned that I have gifts, gifts that were hidden when I focused only on the OCD. I've noticed that I have healing and discernment and wisdom to offer others. I've rediscovered that I'm kind and courageous. Now that I see God clearly I appreciate who God is and who God created me to be! I am a mentor now and God is working through me with my friend. I never let OCD take over who I am now, but I know that will be a life-long struggle.

I think God may be calling me to be a counselor or psychologist so that I can help others through their difficult times.

Ashley shares with passion what God is doing in her life, even in the valley of her struggle with OCD. Her story reminds me of something I say often to students I teach:

"Jesus is not asking us to face anything He hasn't already faced himself. He has faced everything you and I will face, even death, and showed us his power through the resurrection."

I was excited to talk with Ashley because, after not seeing her for a long time, she approached me and told me that Jesus had saved her life. I had to learn more about her story. After talking to her, I discovered that her story is our story: the story of how God saves us from brokenness. Ashley is an incredibly courageous young woman who now understands that no matter what she faces, Jesus will face it with her.

Bringing the Scripture to My Life

- Read "Ashley's Story." What obstacles have made your journey difficult? How has God helped you overcome those obstacles?
- When has something that was not of God begun to define you? How can you reconnect with God during these times?
- Because of the census Mary and Joseph made an unplanned and lengthy journey. What, do you think, were they thinking and feeling as they made the trip from Nazareth to Bethlehem?
- How, do you think, were they able to keep going?
- When have you had a "mountaintop experience"? How did you feel close to God in that moment?
- How have you seen God's light shine in the valleys of life? How have you experienced Christ's power in the midst of difficulty?

Taste and See (Optional)

The video segment for this session features a carob tree. Mary and Joseph likely would have stopped for rest under carob trees on their journey from Nazareth to Bethlehem because the trees provide shade and a sweet snack.

★ LEADERS: Check your grocery store for carobs and carob-based snacks. You may have to go to a store that specializes in health foods or natural foods. Carobs are often used as a substitute for chocolate, so you might also consider baking carob chip cookies.

Video Presentation and Discussion (Optional)

Watch the video segment "From Nazareth to Bethlehem," from *The Journey* DVD. (Running Time: 10:36 minutes)

SIGHTS

- Mount Precipice near Nazareth, the traditional location where Jesus was nearly thrown off the cliff after preaching his first sermon
- The Jezreel Valley, the valley through which invading foreign armies had marched into Israel
- An olive tree grove in the West Bank
- A carob tree that would have provided shade, a place to rest, and food for travelers in Galilee, Samaria, and Judea
- Sychar, where Jesus once stopped to talk to a Samaritan woman at Jacob's well
- The Eastern Orthodox Church of St. Photina, which was built on top of Jacob's well
- The Judean wilderness

KEY INSIGHTS

Mary and Joseph had planned for Mary to give birth in her hometown of Nazareth. Despite Mary being several months pregnant, a census forced the couple to make the journey from Nazareth to Bethlehem, approximately a ten-day walk, where Joseph likely owned land.

Olive oil, from the many olive trees in the Holy Land, was used to anoint high priests and kings.

If Mary and Joseph took the Road of the Patriarchs from Nazareth to Bethlehem, they likely spent the night in Sychar, where there was a water source, Jacob's well. The second half of Mary and Joseph's journey was more difficult than the first. Regardless of their route, they had to travel through dry and desolate land and over many hills and mountains.

This journey, unfortunately, was not the last difficult journey Mary would have to make. She would later have to flee to Egypt and take a trip to Jerusalem that ended with Jesus' death on the cross.

The Bible is full of stories about journeys that people didn't want to take. But God used each of these journeys for God's good purposes. God promises to be present with us, even (and especially) during our most treacherous journeys.

- What do we learn from this segment about the journey that Mary and Joseph had to make from Nazareth to Bethlehem?
- What challenges did Mary and Joseph face along the way?
- How were the places along Mary and Joseph's journey important to Jesus' ministry in later years? How were these places important in the history of the Israelites?
- What difficult journeys have you made? (This could include a journey to the principal's office, a move to a new city, or a trip to visit a loved one in the hospital.)
- How have you been aware of God's presence during these difficult journeys?

Book Study and Discussion (Optional)

Prior to this session, read the fourth chapter, "From Nazareth to Bethlehem," of *The Journey: Walking the Road to Bethlehem*, by Adam Hamilton. Use the following questions to discuss this chapter with your group:

- What did you learn from this chapter about Mary and Joseph's engagement and wedding?
- What did you learn from this chapter about Mary and Joseph's journey from Nazareth to Bethlehem and the routes they might have traveled?
- Why did Mary and Joseph stay in Nazareth after their wedding? Why did they make the trek to Bethlehem even though Mary was so far along in her pregnancy?
- What does this chapter tell us about traditions involving Mary's parents? (Remember that the Bible itself says nothing about Mary's parents. Information about them comes from other sources that were written long after Mary's life and likely are not historically accurate.)
- What was the purpose of the Roman census?
- How, do you think, did Mary react to the news that she would have to make a long journey so near the time she would give birth?
- What landmarks might Mary and Joseph have seen on their journey? Why were these landmarks significant?
- When have you cried out to God in frustration or disappointment? How was God at work during these frustrating and disappointing times in your life?
- What difficult journeys have you made? How did you experience God on these journeys?

Going Deeper in Truth

Scripture includes many examples of God shining light into darkness and bringing hope to people who were traveling through life's valleys. Here are two such examples:

Matthew 9:20-22: Jesus heals the woman suffering from bleeding.
- What difficulties did the bleeding woman face on her journey?
- This story, which also appears in Mark and Luke, is a story within a story. Jesus is on his way to revive a girl who has just died when the woman touches the fringe of his cloak. What does this say about God's ability to provide comfort to all people who are suffering?
- Jesus tells the woman that her faith has made her well. When has your faith made you well? carried you through a tough time?

John 11:1-44. Jesus raises up Lazarus.
- Jesus weeps over the death of his friend Lazarus. What does this moment teach us about God?
- Mary and Martha were in one of life's valleys following the sickness and death of their brother. How did Jesus give them hope?
- By raising Lazarus to life, Jesus shows us what is possible. How does this give all of us hope during difficult times?

Experience Life in Community

Gather in a circle. Think about a time in your life when you experienced God but weren't aware of it at the time. Perhaps God provided you with a friend or an adult whom you could ask for advice. Maybe God helped you keep your composure during an especially stressful time. Or maybe God gave you the strength to turn things around after making a big mistake. Think about how God's light gave you hope during that dark time of your life.

✳ LEADERS: Allow everyone a couple minutes for reflection. Then invite volunteers to tell their stories. Encourage those who are telling their stories to focus on what God was doing and how they experienced God.

Making It Personal

✳ LEADERS: Ask participants to spread out and spend 5–10 minutes of Time Alone with God (TAG). The purpose of this time is for everyone to connect with God personally. Write the following two prompts on a markerboard (or ask the participants to turn to this page in the book):

1. Clear your mind and focus completely on God.
2. Listen for God's voice. Where is God leading you?

After 5–10 minutes of TAG, discuss these questions:

- How difficult was it to clear your mind and focus only on God?
- Is it more or less difficult to focus on God during painful or stressful times in your life?
- How did this time alone with God give you strength and comfort for the journey ahead?

Closing: Listening for God

✳ LEADERS: Gather everyone in a circle and ask them to hold hands. Then ask someone to pray the following prayer:

Holy God, thank you that we are connected to one another in your Spirit. If we find ourselves in the valley, may your strength lift us up and keep us going. Lord, sustain us in our moments of weakness and remind us that we are yours and you are our God. Amen.

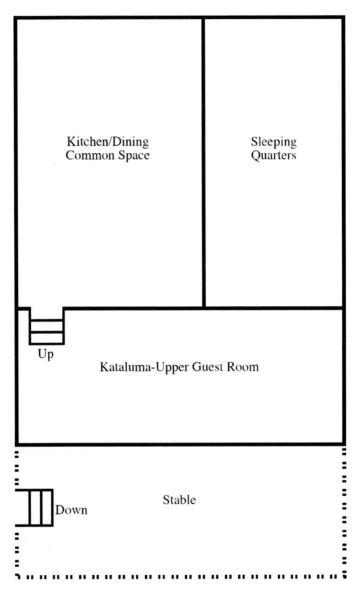

This is a layout of a typical first-century home, such as Joseph's family home in Bethlehem. *Kataluma* is the word in Luke's Gospel that we usually translate as "inn."

Session 5:
This Will Be a Sign to You

Getting Started

Goals for This Session

—Learn that God sent an angel with a message of good news for all people in the birth of the Messiah.

—Discuss the significance of God first giving the good news to lowly shepherds working in the fields at night.

—Learn that we can choose to confess Jesus as Lord and Savior and claim his unconditional love and grace.

—Discover that God speaks to us today through signs and experiences and other people.

Words to Know

Gospel: literally means "good news"—the message of the salvation that we have through Jesus Christ

Testimony: a declaration or proclamation about a belief or experience

Introduction

The angel said, "Don't be afraid! Look! I bring good news to you—
wonderful joyous news for all people. ... This is a sign for you: you
will find a newborn baby wrapped snugly and lying in a manger."
(Luke 2:10, 12)

The angel delivered this message to shepherds. And not just any
shepherds, but shepherds working the night shift. You might
expect such an important announcement to be made to the
king and his court, or to the religious and political leaders in Jerusalem,
or elsewhere in Judea or the Roman Empire. But the angel gave the
message to night-shift shepherds.

In the first century shepherds were usually poor and uneducated and
often smelled like the dirty sheep they tended. The idea that shepherds
were the first people invited to see the Christ Child would have been
shocking to first-century people hearing this story for the first time.

The shepherds were shocked as well. They weren't expecting the Christ
Child to be born at that time, and they certainly weren't expecting angels
to announce his birth to them. Angels were also known to be messengers

of God's judgment, so the sight of an angel would have been terrifying to them. It makes sense that the angel's first words to the shepherds were "Don't be afraid." As the angel proclaimed the good news of Christ's birth and was joined by a multitude singing praises to God, the shepherds' fear turned to joy and excitement.

Here is the entire passage from Luke 2:8-20 about the unlikely night-shift shepherds:

> Nearby shepherds were living in the fields, guarding their sheep at night. The Lord's angel stood before them, the Lord's glory shone around them, and they were terrified.

> The angel said, "Don't be afraid! Look! I bring good news to you— wonderful, joyous news for all people. Your savior is born today in David's city. He is Christ the Lord. This is a sign for you: you will find a newborn baby wrapped snugly and lying in a manger." Suddenly a great assembly of the heavenly forces was with the angel praising God. They said, "Glory to God in heaven, and on earth peace among those whom he favors."

> When the angels returned to heaven, the shepherds said to each other, "Let's go right now to Bethlehem and see what's happened. Let's confirm what the Lord has revealed to us." They went quickly and found Mary and Joseph, and the baby lying in the manger. When they saw this, they reported what they had been told about this child. Everyone who heard it was amazed at what the shepherds told them. Mary committed these things to memory and considered them carefully. The shepherds returned home, glorifying and praising God for all they had heard and seen. Everything happened just as they had been told.

The shepherds had an incredible experience of God, and they had a story to tell. They were eager to tell people what they "had heard and seen." We also have a story to tell. Think about your experiences of God. Was there a single moment when you confessed Jesus as your Lord and Savior? Has your relationship with Christ grown gradually throughout your life? Have there been times when you felt especially close to God or felt that God was at work in your life? How have you told your story of faith? What can people learn about Christ from your story?

Testimony: Kyle's Story

I asked Kyle, who is thirteen years old, to talk about his story of confessing Christ. Here's what he had to say:

JASON: Kyle, when did you take Jesus as your Lord and Savior?

KYLE: It was at summer camp. I was eleven years old, and it was during worship one night. I could feel Jesus' presence in the music and in the room. I could feel God moving me closer and closer. I knew from when I was a kid that God loved me, but it was at that moment I could feel God wanted me to walk closer with God.

JASON: Were you surprised by your experience?

KYLE: Yes, I was. I didn't expect to feel God in that way. I didn't expect that a song could be that moving or that God would meet me right there.

JASON: What did you do next?

KYLE: After the worship we had our cabin group time. I shared with the other guys in my cabin that I gave my life to Jesus. Some of them had done the same thing. It felt pretty cool that I wasn't alone and that those guys also felt God that night.

JASON: Did you tell your parents about it?

KYLE: I shared it with them on the ride home. I told them I saw God like I never had before. When I saw God like I did, I decided to walk with God forever.

JASON: And how are you growing in your walk with God now that you are older?

KYLE: I just went through confirmation and became a member of my church. I memorized The Apostles' Creed and learned what it meant. I think I understand God even more because of that experience. I pray every day, right before bed especially. I think about my goals each day and how they connect with God's goals. I challenge myself to live the fruit of the Spirit, to not be judgmental, and [not to] give in to doubt!

JASON: When you think about Christ as the Savior and Messiah, what comes to mind?

KYLE: I think about what Jesus did for me, how he died for my sins on the cross and took the pain for me.

JASON: How do you, through your faith, show other people who Jesus is?

KYLE: I think about my younger brother. He's eleven years old now, and I think about the example I set for him. I try to love others, to never let my emotions change my faith in God, and to think of others first. You never know what someone might be going through, so I try to be there for him or her however I can.

As I listened to Kyle's testimony, I recognized many signs of God's presence in his story. I saw signs of the Holy Spirit moving through the music when he felt God close, through the outdoor environment of the camp he attended, through his cabin mates as they connected on a shared moment with God, through him retelling the story to his family, through his prayer times, through his decision to be confirmed in the faith, and through his thoughtfulness of others and the example he wants to set for his younger brother.

Kyle's testimony also reminds me that God is moving all around me every day, that God is surprising and amazing, and that God is at work right now!

Bringing the Scripture to My Life

- Read "Kyle's Story." What is your story, or testimony? How have you told people the story about your faith and relationship with Christ?
- The angel told the shepherds that they would see a "sign." What signs have you seen of God's work in your life and in the world around you?
- What "signs" of God have you experienced during this Bible study?
- How does God meet people where they are? In what way does God communicate with people and give people signs?
- God sent an angel to give the good news of Christ's birth to night-shift shepherds. What message, do you think, was God sending

• What does God's choice of shepherds say to us—Christ's followers today—about whom we should serve and to whom we should minister?

Taste and See (Optional)

★ LEADERS: Since this is the final session, celebrate by serving some seasonal snacks. As much as possible, provide snacks that have some connection to the Christmas story. Candy canes are popular at Christmas in part because they resemble shepherds' crooks. Christmas cookies in the shape of a star could represent the star the magi followed, as well as their work as astrologers. Preztel haystacks—pretzels and peanuts covered in melted chocolate then cooled—could represent the hay eaten by the animals that lived in the stable. Peppermint bark, made from crushed bits of candy canes, is an example of taking something broken and making something new. This could symbolize how Christ redeems our broken world.

Video Presentation and Discussion (Optional)

Watch the video segment "The Manger," from *The Journey* DVD. (Running Time: 12:15 minutes)

SIGHTS

• Joseph's hometown of Bethlehem, now a Palestinian city of 40,000 with 200,000 living in the greater Bethlehem area
• The floor plan of a home that might have been similar to the one in which Joseph's family lived
• Manger Square in Bethlehem
• The Basilica of the Nativity, which visitors enter through the Door of Humility (which forces them to bow)

- The Grotto of the Nativity in the Basilica of the Nativity
- The shepherds' fields near Bethlehem
- A current-day shepherd in Bethlehem
- The Chapel of the Manger in the Basilica of the Nativity

KEY INSIGHTS

Mary and Joseph likely were not turned away from an inn (in the "hotel" sense of the word) but were probably unable to stay in the guest room (or *kataluma*) of Joseph's family's home. The stable in which Jesus was born may have been attached to the back of Joseph's family's home, or it may have been a cave underneath the ground on which the home was built.

Shepherds working the night shift were among the lowest of the low in first-century Palestine. Yet these were the people whom the angels first told about the birth of the Messiah.

Mary lay Jesus in an animal feeding trough in a city named Bethlehem, meaning "house of bread." This is appropriate because Jesus is the "bread of life" (John 6:35) who broke bread saying, "This is my body" (Matthew 26:26).

The magi may have been Zoroastrian priests and/or astrologers from Parthia (current-day Iran). They remind us that the good news of Christ's birth was not just for Jews but for all people.

The magi's three gifts were significant: Gold was a gift fit for a king; frankincense was used by priests in the Temple; and myrrh was used for embalming the dead. These gifts anticipated the roles Jesus would play as Savior: He was "king of kings and lord of lords"; he stood in front of God on our behalf like a priest; and he gave his life for us.

- What do we learn from this segment about Jesus' birth? What do we learn about where, and under what circumstances, it happened?

- What does it tell us about God that the first people to learn of Jesus' birth were shepherds working the night shift?
- What do we learn about the life of shepherds from the shepherd interviewed in the video? What do we learn from the shepherd about Jesus' birth and why the angels first told the news to shepherds?
- What do we learn about Jesus from the visit of the magi and the gifts that they brought him?
- What is the significance of Jesus being born in a manger? Why, do you think, was Jesus born in a manger instead of in a palace?

Book Study and Discussion (Optional)

Prior to this session, read the fifth chapter, "The Manger," of *The Journey: Walking the Road to Bethlehem*, by Adam Hamilton. Use the following questions to discuss this chapter with your group:

- What did you learn from this chapter about Jesus' birth? How has reading this chapter changed the way you envision Jesus' birth?
- Why, do you think, do so many Christians visit the Basilica of the Nativity? How do you think it would feel to touch the ground where Jesus may have been born?
- What did you learn from this chapter about the shepherds who first heard the news of Jesus' birth? Why was it significant that the first people to hear this important news were shepherds working the night shift?
- How do you usually envision the multitude of angels who appeared to the shepherds on that first Christmas? How did this chapter change how you picture angels?
- What does it mean for Jesus' birth to be "good news"?
- How do you usually envision the magi, or wise men? How did this chapter change how you visualize the magi?

- Why are the magi so important to the Christmas story? What do they show us about whom Jesus came to save?
- What was the significance of the gifts of the magi (gold, frankincense, and myrrh)?
- What does it mean for Jesus to be the "bread of life"? How does he sustain us and provide us nourishment?

Going Deeper in Truth

Scripture gives us examples of God communicating with people in many different ways. Here are a few passages that show some of the ways that God communicates with people.

Genesis 3:8-21: Even while punishing Adam and Eve for their sin, God shows them a sign of grace.
- How does God give Adam and Eve a sign of love and grace even after they have sinned? (See verse 21.)
- What does this passage tell us about God?

Genesis 9:8-17: God gives Noah the sign of the rainbow.
- What is the meaning of God's sign of the rainbow?
- What does this sign tell us about God's faithfulness?

Luke 2:8-20: God sends a sign by coming in the flesh as a newborn baby.
- We know that Jesus is God in the flesh. We also know that Jesus faced the same temptations and struggles that we do. What does this say about God's love for us?
- What does it mean that God came to us as a baby and was born to a poor family and lay in a manger?

- How have you been—or how will you be—changed by the birth of Christ?
- How will you change the world because of the birth of Christ?

Experience Life in Community

✶ LEADERS: Divide the participants into two teams who will compete in a game of charades. The first team should choose a youth to act out, silently and without using props, the term *Holy Spirit.* Explain that he or she can use techniques such as holding up fingers to indicate the number of words or tugging his or her ear to indicate that a word sounds like another word that is easier to act out. The first team will have one minute to guess the term. If that team is unable to guess correctly, the other team will have an opportunity to steal. Then the second team will select a person to act out the next word (*pastor*). Continue until all the words and phrases have been used. Make sure the teams choose a different representative to play each round. After each round, discuss the question that follows the word or phrase.

1. Holy Spirit
How does God's Holy Spirit speak to us? How do we experience the Holy Spirit?

2. Pastor
How does God speak to us through pastors and other church leaders?

3. Creation
How does God speak to us through God's creation and the natural world?

4. Family

How does God speak to us through our family, our friends, and other loved ones?

5. Teachers

How does God speak to us through teachers (whether at school or at church), through mentors, and through other adults in our lives?

6. The Bible

How does God speak to us through Scripture?

Making It Personal

✶ LEADERS: Ask the participants to take 5–10 minutes of TAG (time alone with God). The purpose of this time is for everyone to connect with God personally. Write the following two prompts on a markerboard (or ask the participants to turn to this page in the book):

- What is God saying to you right now? (Think about all the different ways that God gives us signs and communicates with us.)
- How will you respond to God?

Closing: Listening for God

✶ LEADERS: Gather everyone in a circle and ask them to hold hands. Then ask someone to pray the following prayer:

Holy God, through your love and power you came as a small, fragile child. You faced temptations and death to show us through the Resurrection that your power reigns over all. Open our eyes and ears so that we can see all the ways you are speaking to us and working in our lives. Amen.

A Churchwide Study of
The Journey

✝

The Journey: Walkng the Road to Bethlehem explores the story of Jesus' birth with fresh eyes and ears in an effort to discover the real meaning of Christmas. Author Adam Hamilton draws upon insights gained from historians, archaeologists, biblical scholars, and theologians and from walking in the places where the story occurred.

A churchwide Advent program for all ages will help people come to a deeper understanding of what the Christmas story teaches us about Jesus Christ and about God's will for our lives. It will offer opportunities for learning, for intergenerational activities, and for reaching out to the community.

Resources for the Churchwide Study
ADULTS
- *The Journey: Walking the Road to Bethlehem*—Book
- *The Journey: A Season of Reflections*—Devotional companion
- *The Journey: DVD with Leader Guide*—Videos (optional for youth)

Youth
- *The Journey: Walking the Road to Bethlehem Youth Edition*—Leader Guide

Children
- *The Journey: Walking the Road to Bethlehem Children's Edition*—Leader Guide

Schedule Suggestions

Many churches have weeknight programs that include an evening meal, an intergenerational gathering time, and classes for children, youth, and adults. The following schedule illustrates one way to organize a weeknight program.

- 5:30 P.M.: Gather for a meal.
- 6:00 P.M.: Have an intergenerational gathering that introduces the subject and primary Scriptures for that evening's session. This time may include presentations, skits, music, and opening or closing prayers.
- 6:15 P.M.–8:45 P.M.: Gather in classes for children, youth, and adults.

You may choose to position this study as a Sunday school program. This approach would be similar to the weeknight schedule, execpt with a shorter class time (which is common for Sunday morning programs).

The following schedule takes into account a shorter class time, which is the norm for Sunday morning programs.

- 10 minutes: Have an intergenerational gathering that is similar to the one described above.
- 45 minutes: Gather in classes for children, youth, and adults.

Choose a schedule that works best for your congregation and its existing Christian education programs.

Activity Suggestions

ALL-CHURCH ART SHOW

Directions for an art show can be found in each lesson of *The Journey: Walking the Road to Bethlehem Children's Edition.* Instructions for the final art show are in Lesson 5.

ALL-CHURCH BABY BLANKET DRIVE

Ask participants to bring new baby blankets to give to a homeless shelter, battered women's shelter, or food pantry. If you would like to combine this activity with the previous one, designate the blankets as tickets to enter the art show.

COSTUMED GREETERS

Recruit volunteers to dress up as the biblical characters being studied each week. For the first lesson recruit an adult or youth to dress as the angel Gabriel. Gabriel should greet each person at the door with the words, "Rejoice (person's name), favored one. The Lord is with you!" There are scripts and suggestions for each lesson in *The Journey: Walking the Road to Bethlehem Children's Edition.*

AN AMAZING RACE

Divide the participants into intergenerational groups to play "An Amazing Race." The directions for the game are found in Lesson 3 of *The Journey: Walking the Road to Bethlehem Children's Edition.*

CPSIA information can be obtained at www.ICGtesting.com
Printed in the USA
LVOW030055171111

255327LV00004B/1/P